I0580624

ELIXIR VERSE

EQUINOX

Terra Verses

ELIXIR VERSE EQUINOX
Terra Verses ▽ Spring 2024

A.J.M. Aldrian, Caroline Ashley, James Bosley, C. Brennecke, Audrey T. Carroll, Elayna Mae Darcy, Sean Hanrahan, Maggie Nerz Iribarne, Elizabeth Kerlikowske, Neethu Krishnan, Aimee Lowenstern, Ashling Meehan-Fanning, Dora Morrigan, Christopher R. Muscato, Charlotte Amelia Poe, Christina Rosso, Lorraine Schein, Sarena Tien, Odi Welter, Claudia Wysocky

EDITED BY
C. Brennecke, Elayna Mae Darcy, Christina Rosso

ART BY
Lee Allane, C. Brennecke, Elayna Mae Darcy, Aaron Lelito, Anne Wheeler

www.ElixirVersePress.com

Letter from the Editors

Feel the earth beneath your feet. Let your mind drift away from the mundane. Breathe in the dirt, the leaves, the pollen, the breeze. Feel the sun on your face and remember your childhood wonder; the smell of grass, the feeling of dewdrops soaking through to your knees. Let the physical world speak to you. Its crickets, its birdsong, its whispers, its creaks. Give yourself space to listen; to close your eyes and give in to the moment. You are a child of earth. Your heart belongs with the river and the wild. We all spring to life on this blue sphere together. Our time here is magic. And we hope that you feel its enchantment as you read.

Spells and stories have always mattered to us deeply, and so it feels fitting that our first venture into running an indie publication would find itself at the intersection of both. Because the truth is, they are much the same, spells and stories. Each requires a conjuring of things that weren't there before. Each relies on words in order to exist. And even when the case is a piece of art or a photo that one can only look at, the speaking happens from the art to the soul, sometimes in a way that can't be made tangible, but that doesn't make its communiqué any less real.

This edition, with all its earthen verses, is a meditation on those intersections. The creators included within these pages took our "Terra" prompt and ran in so many different, and beautiful, directions with it. They explored how frozen or broken earth can be deep metaphors for family and buried pasts. They took ancient goddesses of woodland and moon as muses and explored how they could shape their own stories differently from the way the likes of men have mutated them to the public consciousness. Fae folk and burning fires and water spirits abound, all tying back to the open hearted theme of how the natural world is our inherent and collective home.

The essence of life is explored in the margins of these verses, and we could not be more thrilled that these authors and artists have chosen to share with you their tales of heartbreak and hopes. It is our intention as editors, that you may find yourselves in these stories, may see glimpses of dreams yet to be fulfilled, and may answer lingering questions from past wounds. Get lost in these stories of the earth, so that you may find yourself anew.

C. Brennecke

&

Elayna Mae Darcy

Terra Verses ▽ Spring 2024

Blue Ghost Fireflies

by

Neethu Krishnan

Heavenly (G)host, 2021
digital photography,
by Elayna Mae Darcy

An aquamarine fantasy, warm,
beckons. Spun of human desire,
passion-dyed, clipped to hopes
of salvation, folded, preserved
in shelves of hearts,
spooled out and ravaged
in multiverses of art.

Beacon beyond annihilation. Light
before creation. One swaddles
this blanket weaved of the future and
the past, lulled to sleep, rocked to life
in its grandiose cocoon of promises, it may
or may not intend to deliver upon.

This fabric: to hammock, sew
wings golden, bungee
from mediocrity, catapult
to the mythical star. Land right
and an eternity
of radioactive passion—its half-life
a calculated, fickle mystery—is bowled out
in a brilliant flash. Miss, and you still have
your humble earth to fall back on, the glimmer
of a certain celestial yarn
still beckoning, as you go
back to hovering,
a blue ghost firefly over life.

The Cult of Artemis 2.0 on Proxima B

by Lorraine Schein

I, Artemis of the Forest, sure-footed, sharp-eyed,
roaming my moonlit, green-gladed paths on Earth
saw trees scarred by wildfire, uprooted by loggers
the lush canopy of their proud crowns thinned.

My sacred deer and other animals, dying and slain,
my woods, once filled with birdsong,
now silent, slashed through with highways.

When I went to bathe in my sacred spring
dead fish floated on its surface like gray clouds.
The water was blackened by human waste,
slick with oil and bobbing plastic.
Only one blue dragonfly survived, hovering.

I arrowed the mortals who did this—
turned them into prey for my dogs,
then watched with glee as they were devoured.

Even the night sky on Earth was tainted.
The stars scarce. My moon, invaded.
The constellations blurred—
those herds of animals thinned,
and my fellow gods, who once crowded the heavens, scattered.
So I looked to the virgin planets beyond this galaxy for tribute.

Now I am worshipped on new worlds
where I ease the procreation of other beings,
their hatchings and buddings
to create new life, new followers.

In my incarnation here on Proxima B
they pay homage to me, praying:

O Great Artemis 2.0!
Goddess of our exomoons, protectress of wildlife, and nurturer
of our bioengineered forests.
May we not desecrate our forests and world as humans did on
your home planet, Earth.
Nor pollute and contaminate our red skies and yellow seas.
We will honor you in the wild forest of space forever.

The Cherry Blossoms

by A.J.M. Aldrian

      When I was raised, born of the earth
blood-soaked in toil and mirth
because Mother demanded blood for life
and from which I was raised
      blood of frozen white, that melts in the spring sun
      water, blood, for the life of me
      the death of me

      Happy, fatal, sorrow-filled spring
Those freakish curling redwoods—
      spiking up from the earth
      bloody with rainwater dew

Now my flowers flecks are stained
if the Gods bore me pure;
I would retain my whiteness
of spring-melted blood, feminine bed sheets soaked into Mother Earth
      My Father the Sun
raised me unclean, and red strained
flowering pink

I bore my own children, my own fruit,
from which I watched their bloody veins break Mother Earth's ground
and their branches curl up, rising too, big and strong and proud.

      Although their blossoms too, blood red,
        pink faded, left behind and beautiful
        by the sin they all forgot

Now they admire our pinkness,
        as a sign of spring beauty, as they have forgotten how to worship
        Mother Earth and Father Sun
        They've forgotten why
But they still walk our gardens, loving us in the springtime

Not knowing why
they admire us,
what shame they would feel if they did

But Mother Earth demanded blood for birth
She was always beautiful and brutal
They've forgotten how to worship Her, us
        we are just remnants of the past Her
        and our cherry-colored blood,
        we left behind

Note: "The Cherry Blossoms" was previously published in The Afterpast Review.

Persevere 2, 2023
digital photography, by Anne Wheeler

Hard Freeze in the Fruit Belt

by Elizabeth Kerlikowske

Easter egg blue oozes over the Midwest on the weather map.

The forecaster warns us to cover up our plants or bring them in.

Anxiety of commercial growers palpable as a ripe peach, an apricot.

If the blossoms fall, there will be little fruit and little income.

Smudge pots and hope are not enough against the unusual cold.

Frost seems almost welcome, a nuisance, compared to freeze.

In the predawn dark, the growers cup their coffee and wait to see

if the vineyards have been saved by the warmth of Lake Michigan,

if drifts of apple blossoms skirt the trees, and in the next orchard,

if peach blossoms scatter like pieces of mowed-over hose, pink

as dogs' tongues, whose breath makes clouds in the half light of dawn.

The Farm

by dora morrigan

The Farm was built from nothing.

Almost worse than nothing—it was built among the ruins of another life. Monuments of outdated junk were posted in rusted glory where life refused to grow. Any attempt to melt the metal into anything useful would've corroded the inventions into dust. The house in the middle of the property was unlivable, a condemned shack more appropriate for the dynasties of rats that resided in its walls than humans. Not even ghosts wanted to claim the desolated state of the building. The property was a disaster and a waste of land. Of course, the despair harvested from this soil just made it all the more appropriate for my family to plant their roots upon it.

The Farm became my parents' hope and their inheritance for me.

Through incredible trial, they cleared the junk. They tore down the home. They built a new one. Only the desperate would've thought the land possible to rescue, but my parents were bred from perseverance. Both of them were born from farmers who survived impossible conditions across countless generations. Grit grew from their bones through brutal winters that cut through soft skin like scissors on paper. Tenacity laced their blood from the never-ending blistering summers that scorched harvests. My parents were born to survive on land. The earth called to their souls like a chain in a prison cell. But the circumstances of their middle births denied them their birthrights. There was nothing for them to grow. They decided they would create their own home from the ruins of a junkland one way or another. They would create a legacy to pass onto their children bred from the same grit and toil—the children who inherited the same blood sworn to the earth, as the earth is the only reason why they bleed.

The Farm is my parents' hope and their inheritance for me.

It is on The Farm that I find myself in between the spaces of my life, among the ghosts of what used to be and the whispers of what could be. I never wanted this place. I still don't want it. The house is built on the shouts from my mother, the cold shoulder of my father, the misery of my brother, and the cruelty of our past generations' actions to survive the earth. My parents may have cleared physical junk to build their home, but it remains littered with emotional garbage. Where they grow new life, replacing the trash with trees and bees and flowers, I still only see death. Where I crave fire, to burn through what exists and create anew, I am awarded only dust. The Farm is not a home but a cage in which I'm forced to pace the fence line, watching where freedom beckons me but refuses to release me.

The Farm is my inheritance.

This is what my parents built to give me. A farm built from a junkyard. A chance to create sustenance from ruined earth. An opportunity to grow in a land that denies life to its very core. A family created from the earth cannot cut the thick roots that form them. They can only water what's good, prune the diseased, and hope the land will provide in return.

This is my parents' hope and their inheritance for me.

Benediction, 2023
digital art, by Aaron Lelito

Who Haunts Lonely Roads

by Charlotte Amelia Poe

There's no green light across the bay
I sit, feet dangling just above the waterline
Air tinged with salt and the roil of navy clouds above,
And darling, I never believed in love—
If I snatch a firefly out of the gloom,

Cupped gentle in gentle palm, gently, gently

Flicker in and out of a certain glow

You would whisper "crush" and my fingers would twitch—

Uncurl knuckles, uncurl ribs, uncurl the ribbons and tongues you talk

around me

Your eyes are toffee honey brown except at night,

When they turn black and catch the moon like an obscura,

You can be a beautiful liar with your make believe toys,

Shaping me to be one of them—

And your envy shades you, treats you to your ether, and you, you, moth to

flame and expecting me to follow—

I will always lag behind, girl, always drag my feet in the sand

I can't love you, you know?

Thesis statement, now explain

You tell me funhouse mirror fables across radio static

And I mutter, no, no, no, not quite

Sinking below the surface into deepest blue

You paint me every colour you'd like me to be—

So certain, so certain—

That when we collide, we will be ultraviolet—

And shine

And I,

I watch you steal with trapped tongue

Ghost upon ghost

Pale young something boy and draining colder

There's no green light across the bay—

But you say there is, anyway.

An Unmarked Grave

by Odi Welter

You pull the woods child
      out of yourself, reach
           into your chest and find
                their hand, tug them out.
                    They cling to your ribs,
                        clutch your heart, squeeze
                            your lungs until you feel
                      your breath crackle, but you
                cut them out, break them away.
            Your skin tears, heart bruises,
        bones bend, but you drag
them out from their snail-shell home.
      You can't live with them anymore.
        You can't look at them anymore.
            At their round face that mirrors you.
                At their small body that grew into you.
            At the tattered clothes patched with
      wild violets and nettle leaves.
At their scraped knees and berry-stained fingers.
      At the way their eyes hold every story
        you wish you could forget,
            that you plan to bury.

You lead them into the woods
with chickadee calls and honeysuckle flowers
they suckle of their honey.
They leave behind a breadcrumb trail
of touch-me-not pods so you
have a way to find them again.
They help you dig, you call it a game
of make-believe treasure hunting.
They let you turn them into the treasure,
blanket them in the pages of fairy tales,
seal the bark sheath casket,
cover them with soil and moss.
You leave them waiting
for a prince to kiss them alive.

"Heaven and Hell„

by Claudia Wysocky

Silence fills the air,
as I sit, alone,
among endless rows of graves.

I wish for heartbeats,
for laughter,
for tears.

I miss the noise.

But I know that I can't have it.

I can hear the footsteps of the living,
but there's no sound for me.

Silence surrounds me,
as I lay in my own void,
a void of life,
eternal and silent.

I will never know happiness again.

But I accept it,
lying here, alone,
among endless rows of graves.

It was fun being dead for a while,
to feel the quiet
and the peace.
I thought hell would have fire and brimstone,
but I guess that's only what they tell us.

I'm moving on now,
accepting my reality.
And I know that one day,
I'll find my meaning,
in the cold abyss.

But for now, all I have is silence,
a silence that never ends.

And I bet there's fire in heaven.

Shades of Green

by Sarena Tien

The needle doesn't hurt as much as I thought it would. At its worst, it feels like a cat scratching at my leg. The rest of the time, it feels more like a vibration than a sharp point piercing my skin, and only the buzzing sound reminds me that there's a needle.

I didn't know if it would, but getting my first tattoo has paralleled my experience with grief. On my worst days, the loss of my brother hurts more than a cat clawing at my skin, but other days, the ache subsides into a hollow that I've learned to live with.

I chose to mark my upper right thigh because while I'll always know the tattoo is there, it's hidden from other people unless I decide to show them. It's like telling people I used to have a sibling—the wound is there, known only to me, and no one knows it exists unless I diverge from my half-lie of being an only child. I know strangers are only trying to make conversation when they ask if I have any siblings, but my loss is a private pain, and sometimes honesty results in more uncomfortable questions. Saying that I'm an only child isn't untrue if we discount the first twenty-two years of my life.

The dark ink of the tree mirrors the strokes of the brush that my brother once held as he'd painted the trunk and branches onto a sheet of rice paper. After he'd passed away, I'd known that I'd wanted a tattoo, but I hadn't known what design to get until years later, when my eyes had fallen on his sketchbook. I'd flipped through the pages and then grabbed my phone, swiping through other pieces of his art until one work caught my eye. In the Chinese watercolor painting, two birds hover above a tree, and although he'd painted the piece in elementary school, it'd been a winning contest entry.

I'd made one change in translating his art into a tattoo: replacing the yellow leaves with green ones, partly because my skin already carries yellow undertones, and partly because green was his favorite color.

"We're finished," the tattoo artist announces, and I prop myself up on my elbows, studying the tree on my thigh.

We admire the piece together. The green watercolor base complements the vibrant leaves at the top of the tree, anchoring the whole piece in a feeling of symmetry.

"I'm really glad you asked me about adding green at the bottom," I say, because I'd originally just been considering a tree without grass.

"I agree," the tattoo artist says. "The green at the bottom really balances the piece and brings everything together."

Although I still feel like the funeral home buried both of us on that rainy day in May seven years ago, as I look down at my tattoo, I realize the tree growing out of the grass embodies all the contradictions of grief; it's a graveyard and a garden, an entanglement of the past and the future, an executioner and an epilogue.

Two weeks ago, a friend asked, "Why not one of the birds?" and I shrugged, unable to explain why I'd been drawn to the flora rather than the fauna.

Now, tracing the bends and bows of the tree's branches over the clear medical bandage, feeling the slight twinge of pain that follows the pressure of my finger, I know that a part of me did die the day of my brother's funeral.

But another part of me will rest forever rooted to him. His death has also become a source of life, nudging me to figure out who I am with and without him.

The Poem I Will Never Write

by Ashling Meehan-Fanning

you tried to bury it
in the garden
among ferns and bones
but it came back up
its boots sticking out of the dirt
a roguish smile on its face. you
tried digging deeper,
tried spells and the tricks
your mother taught you
but each night the moonlight licks
its bare, uncovered face its eyes
staring up at your bedroom
window, its voice echoing like
latent thunder, like deep
rumbling of the earth's core,
when it asks *why*.

The Wind is Buddha

by James Bosley

Go outside
because the wind is Buddha
Remove those headphones
because the birds are Buddha
Toss away your cap
the sun itself is Buddha
Take off your shoes, your socks
yes the grass is Buddha

the rough feel of the red oak bark
the smell of earth heavy after rain
the perfect laughter of a child
all of these
all of these
all of these
and you as well.

Persevere 2, 2023
digital photography, by Anne Wheeler

Pass

by James Bosley

Deep down the field he hurls
a long, long arcing pass
that grazes off the fingertips
of his older self
incomplete

The Seven Sages of Grief

by Christopher R. Muscato

1.   Salvia dorrii: Perennial spreading shrub, grey-green leaves; needs well-drained, dry soil

The body is complete, 3D-printed biofilament wires braided into a usable frame around the well-loved mountain bike. Atop the frame has been placed a fine mesh, hardened like plaster with a nutrient-rich brine. And then the carefully sculpted, soil-supporting lattice into which all the other elements would be grafted.

But these things didn't just happen. The mesh didn't fold itself, didn't paint itself with the solvent. The lattice didn't shape itself, and as for the shrubs; they didn't plant themselves, prune themselves into an almost bonsai-like state, graft themselves onto the frame. There were hands that did these things. Hands that should still be here.

"Desi, everything alright?"

"I'm fine, just a thorn," Desi mumbles, her attention shifting back to the crimson dot on her thumb. She sucks away the blood and returns to her work. Not that it matters. It won't change anything. Desi continues grafting the budding branches of desert sage onto the frame. A drop of bioengineered amino solvent to secure it. A drop more. A drop of crimson. Desi sucks the wound on her thumb again.

There is one bud that has flowered early. Desi rubs the purple petals, then senses the minty aroma in her nose as she crushes them between her fingers.

2.		*Salvia sonomensis: Mat-forming subshrub, variable color, easy to cultivate*

The frame of the bicycle is still evident beneath the greenery, but just barely. It looks like it will hurt to ride. Maybe that's what she wants. The thought pierces Desi with guilt.

Stop making it about you, Desi scolds herself, refocusing. The desert sage has accepted the grafting. Next comes the Sonoma sage, *Salvia sonomensis*, a creeping sage. Once established, it will spread over the entire bicycle. It's an obvious choice, perhaps, but one *she* had made. In fact, it was one of the last she had made. Or, at the very least, the last that made any sense. Desi wasn't there when her sister chose to stray from the path.

Desi stiffens at the hand on her shoulder. Hanako offers her a weak smile, and Desi reciprocates. The guilt returns. She isn't the only one dealing with this. Hanako, obviously, but Carver, Ruth, Carl, Janaki too. Perci's comrades in horticulture. The Southern California Tour de Flor is their annual tradition, Desi is just filling in. A placeholder.

She feels the mist in her eyes and tries to push the pain, the guilt to the back of her mind, but it returns, creeping.

3.		*Salvia carduacea: Strong citronella aroma, spikey (ouch!), flowers grow on spiny calyces*

Grafting *Salvia carduacea* onto the hedge of a bicycle is not too difficult, but would be easier without all the noise. Desi scrunches her face, trying to concentrate on pruning, trying to ignore the heat rising in her cheeks.

"But not before she got caught vandalizing the country club with…

what was it?" Carver's laughter echoes off the photovoltaic panels of the greenhouse.

Christianopoulos, Desi snaps, in her mind.

"That quote she loved, about trying to bury us, but we were seeds." Ruth's head pops up from behind her own bicycle, ornamented lavishly in soon-to-blossom California poppies.

"And then seed bombing the golf course! She almost got us all arrested!"

Like any of you really knew. You weren't there when the elders taught us we could use gardening to reclaim what was taken.

"Perci sure was something." Hanako's voice is soft, like a prayer. Desi buries her head deeper into the sage she is pruning.

"Desi," Janaki calls. "I'm sure you've got plenty of stories. Take a break, join us."

"No thanks," Desi grumbles. Her voice is low, but her fingers shake. To hear her sister's friends, even Hanako, telling stories…laughing…

Desi hears her heartbeat in her ears, feels her pulse in her temples, the grating of her teeth, and then—

Snap

Desi stares in horror at the broken handlebar. She didn't realize… she didn't mean to…

A strangled scream escapes her lips and instantly she is surrounded.

"Fixable." Carl cradles the splintered branches. "Ruth, grab me the chlorobinder. Carver, a biofilament patch?"

As the others scuttle about, all Desi can do is stare.

"Don't worry. It happened to Perci all the time." Hanako's voice seems to echo, distant in Desi's ears. And then, "It will be okay."

So complete is her outrage, all Desi can do is storm out of the greenhouse, leaving behind pots of thistle sage still waiting to be grafted onto the bicycle.

4.   *Salvia leucophylla: Aromatic shrub with allelopathic qualities, drought tolerant*

Desi's breath is heavy, the sweat on her neck is cold, and her muscles burn. She places a foot on the ground, bringing the bike to a rest. Her street bike is not suited for this terrain. Unable to let herself borrow one of Perci's many off-roaders, however, Desi has no other choice. She takes a gulp of water, surveys the hills.

Not a person in sight. Ever since she got here, she's been drowning in a flood of people, all the time. But this isolation is freeing. She could vanish and nobody would see a thing, nobody would notice. She would simply disappear.

She begins to pedal again. Perci's parade bike is still in the greenhouse, handlebar repaired, and recently augmented with purple sage. Desi likes working with that one. It feels right. *Salvia leucophylla*, according to Perci's notes, releases a chemical that prevents any plants sharing its soil from growing. As the path winds through the bluffs, Desi imagines what it would be like to put down roots somewhere far away and salt the earth around her.

Why is she even doing this, she wonders, building her sister's parade bicycle for the stupid procession, the Tour de Flor, this garish cavalcade her sister and her stupid friends do every year? Maybe she'll just leave, go anywhere else, where nobody knows her, knew her sister, knows—

Gravel scatters under the tires as Desi squeezes the brakes. Though the path is flat, her breaths come in forceful gasps. Her chest broils in flames. Ahead, the route curves east around a large bluff. Branching off this, west towards the ocean, lies a barely visible side trail with yellow caution tape still draped across it. Wilted bouquets litter the ground.

Desi races away, intent on leaving. These bluffs, this city, all of it.

5.   *Salvia apiana: Evergreen shrub, attracts bees as pollinators (*Ask elders abt uses)*

Desi clenches the white sage in her fist and stares at the bluff. Just that morning she found the *Salvia apiana* flourishing on the parade bike. It wasn't looking good the day before. She didn't think this round of grafting would take.

Something about the white sage's presence, its resilience, haunts her. Desi takes a deep breath and leans her bike on its kickstand next to the yellow caution tape.

Hands shaking, Desi climbs the hill until she feels her hair whip in the salty wind, hears the rumbling of waves pounding her ears. She draws a sharp breath and looks out over the ocean, wind and tidal turbines dotting the horizon.

The mist of sea breeze speckles Desi's cheek, followed by the stinging of tears. Desi squeezes her fists. She takes a breath, and looks down.

At the base of the bluff, a faint trail ends abruptly; a gaping wound torn into the cliffside where a large section has simply fallen away.

Perci cared so deeply about restoring this coastline, repairing the damage done by generations before who let the planet burn. Her rewilding campaigns helped stabilize these cliffs, native roots holding together the depleted soil, but the work isn't done. Even with the drought over, decades of damage are carved into the terrain like a crypt.

Desi stares at the hole that swallowed her sister. One finger opens from her fist. Then another. Another. She releases the white sage and watches it drift away.

Hours later, Desi returns to the greenhouse. Her sister's friends are there. Desi quietly starts working alongside them, misting the miraculous white sage on her sister's parade bicycle. Hanako retreats to the workbench, and Desi slips after her.

"I went to the cliffside today," Desi whispers, fidgeting with a pruning kit.

"Then you did something I haven't been able to," Hanako admits. She smiles weakly. Desi hesitates, then reaches out to touch Hanako's hand. The hand that had held her sister's, that still wears her sister's engagement ring.

"Maybe we can go together."

6.   *Salvia mellifera: Perennial shrub, turns dark during drought, grows in many soils*

There is more than enough black sage left in the pots. Perci planted a surplus in preparation for some of the grafting to fail, which now turns out to have been an unnecessary precaution. Desi snips off a few handfuls of leaves and stems. Hanako winces as she removes her boots.

"My feet are killing me," she says.

"Same." Desi sprinkles the clippings into a pitcher of water and places it in the sunlight. She drops into a folding chair. "Let that steep for a few hours. Black sage sun tea is a natural painkiller."

"What do we do? Drink it?"

"We soak our feet in it." Desi laughs. She catches herself. The laugh is a surprise. It doesn't feel right, something so bright poking through the darkness. Still, it has made it through.

"How'd you learn this?" Hanako ignores the pause, which Desi appreciates.

"Our grandmother. She and the other elders taught me and Perci about native plants."

"Perci talked about that a lot," Hanako says, voice trailing off as some memory pushes its way forward.

Leaving Hanako to her thoughts, Desi's attention drifts to the parade bicycle. What was once a frame and mesh is now a veritable topiary of sage varieties, nearly ready to bloom. That was Perci's design for the Tour de Flor native plant bicycle parade. As they pedal along the trail, bits of the bicycles will fall away, a jubilant marathon of carnivalesque gardeners seeding the land.

Black sage darkens during drought, according to Perci's notes. The *Salvia mellifera* of their childhoods only grew very dark. But this sage growing on the bicycle is lighter.

"Think you'll stick around after the parade?" Hanako's voice shakes Desi out of her trance. Desi shrugs, but her mind flashes with images that feel forbidden, visions of a life she could have here.

"You've got a talent for this," Hanako says. "We'd be happy to open a spot for you in our very exclusive horticultural club."

Desi laughs. It still doesn't feel right, but it feels less wrong than before. Desi looks again at the black sage. Not all things that seem dark forever remain that way.

7.   *Salvia spathacea*

The bicycle is simply alive. It is bursting in colors, blue and red and purple and white petals among silver-green leaves. Desi's eyes linger on the soft lilac of the hummingbird sage, the final variety grafted into this mobile bouquet.

Desi smiles as she feels Hanako's hand on her shoulder.

"Ready?" Hanako asks.

"As I'll ever be."

Along with the rest of Perci's friends, they make their way to the parade route at the foot of the bluffs. What was a parking lot has transformed into a wondrous garden. A boisterous agave-themed bike sits next to one covered in bonzai-style manzanitas. Another is almost indiscernible under a mountain of blue-green wild rye, shaking in the breeze like some mythical, lumbering beast. Everywhere, grasses quiver and branches rustle, sunlight glistens off waxy leaves, and the sweet aroma of flowers saturates the salty, coastal air.

Hanako sniffles. Desi follows her gaze to a towering memorial on which is written, in flowers:

Dedicated to a Tour de Flor Founder

Who Believed Planting a Garden was the Purest Kind of Hope:

Perséfone Konoyo Shalawa

"Damn, Perci would have loved that spotlight."

Desi wraps Hanako in a hug, laughter bubbling through tears. When they pull apart, Desi feels a warmth she had forgotten she was capable of feeling.

Desi turns to her bike and sees a hummingbird jumping from flower to flower. The hummingbird perches on the sage and is still for barely a moment, but it is long enough for Desi to smile at it, to tell her sister that she loves her, and that she'll be alright.

The hummingbird flits away and Desi mounts the bike, proudly taking her sister's place among the sages.

Persephone, 2006
oil on canvas, by C. Brennecke

Ballad

by Ashling Meehan-Fanning

I met a god in Gallistel Woods.
The longer I walked, the more she spoke to me
through the wind and the dirt and the animal bones
buried beneath the ground, she said:
      go further go further go further

So further I went into Gallistel Woods
and came upon a barren beehive,
vacant and deserted beneath the arms
of a burr oak tree. A hundred hollow eyes
stared back at me, the formidable entrance
into a queen's lair now abandoned.
I paused at the trunk of that burr oak tree
and waited for god to speak:
      go further go further go further

Soon I arrived at a vast empty field
outside of Gallistel Woods, the grass
browned and flattened by winter's glare.
A solemn pine stood sentry and swayed
with the god's commanding voice:
      go further go further go further

To my knees I knelt then in prayer
and laid upon my back, I praised.
God sent her hands through the ground,
into my hair, wrapped fingers through
my red braid, held me tight. I closed my eyes,
listened for the sweet whisper:
       go further go further go further

In the grass outside of Gallistel Woods, I dreamt of empty homes and
vacant cities. I dreamt of vines thrust between tire tracks, sidewalk cracks. I
dreamt of trees growing tall in alleyways and basketball courts. I dreamt of
maggots pillaging what remains, of humanity seeking solace underneath the
wide-reaching arms of a burr oak tree.

I dreamt of what the god whispered to me. I felt her joy.

Hold My Ashes, 2021
digital photography, by Elayna Mae Darcy

Even in the Embers

by

Elayna Mae Darcy

We were both tried by fire
in the softest of ways.

We were not thrown,
howling into a blaze
that would seek to teach us
that the only road to success
must be one paved in suffering.

Together we learned
we could be marshmallows,
gently toasting and cozy
while we lose ourselves to
the campfire songs
and longing tales
that others had to spin.

We reached within,
where we found that
kindness can be fiery too—
warm and inviting,
teaching us by the light
to love & find beauty
even in the embers.

Heavenly Virginity

by Christina Rosso

CW: mentions of sexual assault and harassment

It isn't true that I asked my father, Zeus, for eternal virginity. It wasn't that I was prude or disinterested in the pleasures of the body. I didn't wish for eternal life, untouched by love and passion.

It is true that I wished for one thing in particular: to be untouched by man, by their prickly, ravenous hunger. I had seen the way both mortal men and gods gorged on women, licking and sucking and ripping flesh and bone until their bodies were conquered and unwound. Deflated into empty sacks of skins.

I witnessed it happen to my mother, knowing how my father pursued first my aunt, Asteria, who threw her body into the sea to avoid his assault, and then turned his eyes to my mother, Leto, the gentlest of all the Titans. My mother would never tell me the details of her *pollination*, as I referred to it. I wanted to call it what it most likely was, what it always was with the king of the gods, but every time her face stopped me, its soft oval shape sharpening, her chin trembling, her always smiling lips rolled out to a thin line. No, I couldn't bring her to such sadness. Such truth. She had endured enough from my stepmother, Hera, having been tormented and exiled by the goddess to wander the lands for a peaceful place to give birth to her twins.

My mother is the titan goddess of motherhood and childbirth. Legend has shaped her into an ideal—the perfect, doting mother—a representation of how we women are supposed to be. This legend has inspired new tales from old skins, such as the story of a princess embraced while she sleeps, her body an incubator for nine months until two babies, a boy and a girl are born. The boy is named for the sun, the girl for the moon. Only when one of the nursing infants mistakes her finger for a breast, does the princess awaken. She is overjoyed at her new role, never questioning the violation it reflects, embracing motherhood with ease. A natural, they would say today.

I've never wanted to be confined by man's image, a one-dimensional ideal. I've never wanted to be like my mother, chased from one land to the next, my belly distended with the fruits of infidelity and trespass. I've never wanted to be violated like that, scooped out until I am nothing but a hollow carcass.

Gender roles have always seemed too limiting to me. I am both a mother of the wilderness and a father of the hunt. I have breasts, yes, yet still, I shoot the deadliest arrows in both the heavenly and earthly realms. I assist with childbirth and protect pregnant folks. I walk in step with nature. You've likely seen my kin of stags, their hooves leaving faint prints in the mud, their snacking leaving holes in your greens. Maybe you've even heard the howling of my kin of hounds prowling beneath the dark moon.

My myth has a common misconception—that being untouched by man means I possess heavenly virginity. That the only way to make love or fuck involves a dangling appendage. I assure you I have experienced both pleasure and comfort with nymphs, goddesses, and even mortal women. The earth is a sensual entity, and I honor its rhythms.

Society fears natural rhythms, anything that is not regulated by its male keepers. It's the same with the gods. One of the greatest mysteries of the world is that women, and those with uteruses, can bleed once a month without dying. It makes this faction of the population god-like, and therefore, dangerous. Empires have always feared powerful women, regardless of whether ambrosia courses through their veins or not. Legends are born out of this fear as warnings to femme-folk.

It's true, I've slain men who have violated me. My hands dripped with their blood. And yet. The true story has never been told before now.

Of course, this is because the inventor of the tale was my father, Zeus, the worst kind of chauvinist. He wanted all of his daughters to be eternal virgins, not just me. He was allowed to toss and thrust his seed throughout the realms with no recourse. But his daughters, no, they were supposed to be as chaste as priestesses. The irony, of course, is that chastity invites lust. My uncle, Poseidon, violated Medusa, a priestess in my sister, Athena's, temple. Her purity created an obstacle that my uncle needed to overcome. We all know what happened to Medusa, don't we?

Perhaps that's why my father invented the myths surrounding Actaeon and Orion. Perhaps it was his way of saying there would be pain for anyone who violated his kin. I suppose I should be flattered. My father rarely shows his children this level of attention, and yet. Why should he get to shape my story?

I think it's time I tell my truth.

The summer sun scorched the earth, leaving the grass brown and brittle, the flora withering and the beasts panting on their sides. I rose with my cousin, Eos, the rosy hues of dawn stretching as far as the eye could see, and disappeared into the mouth of the woods to hunt. I returned with a couple of hares to roast for breakfast. I have never believed in having priestesses who worship me by erecting a temple in my honor. In my father's version of the stories, my companions are always virgins. In truth, some of them are virgins by choice. Others simply don't hold any interest in being brides and mothers. Can you blame them?

A community without the wandering eyes and roaming hands of men is a sacred one. We live modestly, in harmony with the land and its creatures. There is no hierarchy. We are individuals who together form a sisterhood. We leave the shame of mankind in our villages and the kingdom of the gods and enter the wilderness liberated. We hunt and forage together, cook and bathe together, and some of us couple together. There are no limitations in the natural world. Just our bodies, our essences, and the cycles of the land.

During the summer, when the sun reaches its peak in the clouds, its rays stretching from the earthly realm to the heavens, my sisters and I slip into the river nearby our camp. We let the rushing water heal our muscles and replenish our spirits. We swim and play and float, a respite from the day's labors. On one such afternoon, a hunter tracking a stag with his pack of hounds came upon my sisters and me in the river. His name was

Actaeon, as I would later learn from the story my father wove. I wouldn't give him the chance to introduce himself.

The young hunter hid behind a tree, spying on us, while his dogs wandered up to the water to drink. We greeted the dogs as we greet all of nature's beasts, our palms outstretched in welcome. But we weren't empty headed maidens incapable of recognizing the nearby voyeur. Many of my sisters sank lower into the water to cover their nudity. I rose from the river, goosebumps covering my naked curves. I wanted to distract the hunter, before bringing him to heel. Something I learned from my sister, Aphrodite.

"You can come out," I said to Actaeon, my voice saccharine.

He stepped out from the tree with a rustle. I eyed the undone ties of his pants, evidence of his enjoyment. His face turned a brilliant red as he saw me notice his erection.

"Like what you see?" I said, gesturing to my body.

He stared at me, stunned. To this day, I can't be sure if he recognized me or if a naked woman speaking to him in such a confident manner was too shocking.

"Do you like to watch women without their permission?"

"I—" he started.

I held my hand up to silence him. "Do you think we exist for your enjoyment?"

"I was out on a hunt when I found you," he managed to say.

"And instead of making your presence known, you hid behind a tree and pleasured yourself?"

He chewed on his lips, his face growing redder.

"Women have been hunted by men since creation. Like stags, we try to escape your gaze and your grasp. And yet, even when we leave our villages, we cannot escape you. You track and violate us in our new home. I think it's time you learn what it's like to be the hunted."

He went to speak when his mouth and nose stretched into a muzzle. His body fell forward, hooves catching his fall instead of hands and feet. Two fur-covered ears twitched at the surrounding sounds. I whistled to the hunter's hounds and said one word: "Fetch."

The dogs bounded after their master, now a stag darting through the woods that only moments before he had been the deadliest predator of.

At the time, I didn't think much of the story this would lead to or how it might draw the attention of other men, hungry for a piece of the goddess of the hunt and her companions. I thought of my sisters, of my lovers, and their safety. We had worked to create a safe community, with respect and autonomy as the core tenets. I promised myself I wouldn't let another infiltrate our home.

Summer slipped into fall, rust and tawny leaves concealing the path to our community. I continued to rise at dawn and hunt for our meals. On warmer days, we still bathed in the river to cool off. On other days, the chill in the air made us fasten our capes and huddle together for warmth by the fire. We worked to prepare a cave just outside of the woods for the winter, storing provisions of salves, herbs, and meat.

On the eve of the full moon, known as the Hunter's Moon, the hunter known as Orion found his way to our cave. For hours, he hid, waiting stone-still in the brush so as to not give himself away. My sisters and I used the luminescence of the pregnant moon to hunt, one final chance to build up our stores for winter. We arrived back at the cave late and fell into heavy slumbers. I remember dreaming about Actaeon, still in the form of a man, being chased by his beloved hounds. It was a reverie of comfort, a way for my mind to assure me we were safe. Now I look back on that dream as a warning of the danger that lurked just beyond our cave.

I woke to a blade against my throat. He didn't say a word, yet I knew from his agitated breathing what he pursued. Women have been the prey of men like Orion since Prometheus shaped the first of humankind out of clay. It isn't a new story, but an ever-important one. Women's bodies are sacred and our boundaries should be honored.

You might be wondering why I even hesitated to destroy this hunter. As a goddess, I am impervious to death. But that doesn't mean I am impervious to trauma, nor that my sisters were free of my Uncle Hades's skeletal grasp. I would not let Orion violate me in our home. I wouldn't let my sisters be subjected to any more horrors. I reached behind my back to his erection. Cupping it, I whispered, "Outside. Under the moon."

He kept the knife against my gullet as he led me outside. "Over there," I said as we neared the entrance to the woods.

I could feel the fury in his hands and groin, how they trembled with the anticipation of taking the virgin goddess of the hunt. Orion shoved me onto the ground, my palms and knees scraping against fallen branches. I gazed up at the moon, at its fiery glow. The moon has always given me strength and wisdom. Closing my eyes, I pictured one of the most dangerous hunters. A low hiss rushed the solitude of the woodlands. I remained on my hands and knees, knowing what was about to transpire.

"What the—?" the hunter said before howling in agony.

I looked over my shoulder at him then, his Achilles tendon caught in the pincer of a giant scorpion. "Hello, friend," I said to the creature as it curled its tail to inject venom into my hunter.

The poison swam under Orion's skin, a faint glow emanating like a constellation twinkling in the sky. His eyes bulged, drool dribbling from his mouth. "Did you know the October full moon is also known as the Blood Moon?"

Crimson tears slipped down Orion's face.

"It was foolish of you to go after the goddess of the hunt when this moon was at its apex. Its power radiates through me, inspiring the hunted to take back our power. Like the great scorpion, we are predators."

Wisps of gray and black strands rose from Orion's body, his soul leaving his body. "Say hello to Hades for me," I said before his body dropped to the ground and turned to dust.

No man has dared trespass on our land since. We rested that winter, and with Spring's rosy embrace, we began to heal. To live without looking over our shoulders at every snap or growl in the woods. As you can see, I never asked my father, Zeus, for eternal virginity, nor for the tales he spun about my assailants. I never yearned for a life of eternal frigidity. All I wanted was to be safe from the gluttony of men.

Together, my sisters and I have built a sanctuary for those who want to live beyond the trappings of the patriarchy. There are no expectations for those in our community to become wives or mothers or have their bodies be used for anything other than their personal pleasures. We live in tandem with the earth and its pulses, drawing strength from its beasts and its flora. And that certainly seems heavenly to me.

Perception, 2022
digital photography, by Elayna Mae Darcy

Perceived, 2022
digital photograph, by Elayna Mae Darcyy

Nesting Doll

by Aimee Lowenstern

I nearly don't go on a walk today, distracted as I am
by the biomes of my skin, the cool morning air diminished
in places by the heat of a nearby vein or the grace of a sunbeam—

(The sun larger than all imagining, brighter than any pain,
a yarn-ball of fire spun round and round
longer than history, though perhaps not longer
than the threaded nerves of every living thing)

Does the world feel its roots-stems-trunks
the way I feel the million tiny
hairs across my body, the way I feel
the fur of my taste buds as I move my tongue
over slightly-scalloped teeth, thinking of the
endless-though-eventually-ending mycelium
under where my legs split and bend, thinking of
the worms, that taste as much as touch,
brushing against each sparkling-and-not-sparkling
fleck of dirt, their flesh shining brown and pink
like lengths of smoky rose quartz?

(The clouds may come down
and bring the worms up soon,
acres of sky-water misting
over hills squamous with evergreens,
each mammoth branch
blurred to nothing by distance.)

The ground is cross-stitched with pine needles,
sequined with aspen leaves.
I am so busy looking for the whole picture
that I almost miss the bear

crossing   the   path   in   front   of   me.

The Danger of Listening to the Cars

by Sean Hanrahan

I want to live in the lyrics of a Cars song
Synth my way to heaven
Exfoliate my skin on Ric Ocasek's vibrato
Get lost in his cool shades
Glam myself up for Tuesday night
Head outside into the Miami Vice scent
Slow roll brush fellow pastels
Cover my cold shoulders
with my boyfriend's Members Only jacket
Tie myself in knots with his skinny tie
You're all I got tonight
Forget about AIDS for a while

Coyote

by

Sean Hanrahan

I walked out into the coyote's howl
Waiting to be devoured
Life had nothing to offer me
I had lost all my power

I walked out into the coyote's howl
Heedless of the hour
There was no one left I wanted to be
My soul could not reflower

I could not awaken from this dream
Desolate, suicidal, sour
Limbs trapped by a heavy weight
The coyote knew this and glowered

The coyote growled, circled me twice
Weary hungry jaws poised to snap
I remembered to call it by its former name
It bowed and nuzzled my unseated lap

After some time, this creature skulked away
Springing itself from my subtle trap
I decided I could survive another day
But I could always call the coyote back

The Kelpie

by Caroline Ashley

I roam the moors like a dispossessed phantom. I dream of a land I never knew, where comfort and security spill forth from the soil.

Summers here bring the moors to life with heather. Ptarmigan and hares bound through the rocks with me and we chase each other. We revel in the open-skied freedom, though the razor-sharp cliffs are never far from mind. When winter sets in, the wind is our enemy. It sweeps across the village, as relentless as the thundering waves crashing against the shore below. I shelter at home with my family, huddled by the dried peat fire, seeking comfort in the dark.

On those cold nights, Da prays at his bedside, whispering hopes to the Lord, while Ma lays a cup of milk at the door, to ward off the fair folk. "The Lord may protect us," she would say, "but the fae dinnae listen to prayers."

As I walk through the moors one cool spring morning, winter relaxing its deathly hold on the terrain, a movement draws my eye to the burn.

I see a man. A chiselled square face, pink rosebud lips, skin damp with dew. Black hair falls in a glistening wave to his shoulders. He lifts his head, tossing the tresses to reveal steel-silver eyes that pin me in place like a mouse in a trap.

My heart scrabbles for purchase, trying to escape his sights. My arms rise to my chest, as if fragile flesh could defend me. I swallow bile and step backward.

My eyes scour the path to the settlement, but I am alone. When my gaze returns to the man, he has become a shining black stallion, nostrils flaring as he huffs out a breath. His tail cuts through the air and he stamps a rounded hoof against stone.

"Mercy," I whisper and drop to my knees, head bowed.

A sudden thud draws my eyes upward. The horse lays on his side, chest rising and falling in a hurried beat. I hesitate—trapped in the moment like a deer catching sight of a bow. When he doesn't rise, I take a step forward.

"Kelpie," I say. The word is a petal on the breeze, spoken so softly my own ears struggle to catch it.

He hears. He lifts his head and tosses his neck. Muscles strain to stand, his limbs trembling and mouth straining for breath. His eyes turn to the burn, as if willing it to flow in his direction. Somehow he is injured, severed from the safety of his realm. The preacher would call him an emissary of the devil. The godly thing would be to abandon him, return to my home and pray for my immortal soul.

He closes his eyes, accepting his fate. I share the sentiment. I wonder if the earth has expelled him to the ends of the land too.

My father used to farm at Ausdale but he and Ma were evicted before I was born, sent here to rebuild their lives on the sea while the land they used to till made way for livestock. Sheep are worth more than we are.

Others abandoned the Highlands entirely, setting sail for the new worlds, in hope of re-growing the roots they'd lost. Da wouldn't hear of it— *Scotland's ma hame*, he'd say. *They cannae tak' that frae me.*

Camaraderie compels me to action. I reach into my apron pocket for a handkerchief. I run to the burn and bathe the fabric in water, dripping a trail of ice-cold liquid across the grass before running it across his brow. He closes his eyes, embracing the touch of the cloth.

His stillness makes me brave. Trembling fingers stroke his side, the surface smooth as silk and warm as a rock in the summer sun. His muscles relax beneath my fingers.

Thunder rumbles and the first drops of rain strike my head. I hear my name drifting across the moors. His steel eyes watch me, waiting for my next move. I rise and back away, only turning to run home when certain he won't chase after me.

He is my shadow in the months of spring and early summer, gleaming flanks drawing my eye as I venture through the moors. He stands tethered to the burn, water caressing his fetlocks. I dare not touch him, fearful of being swept to a watery grave. Sometimes I lift my hand, tracing a path over his muzzle, never quite connecting with flesh. They say you cannot trust the fae. They haunt our lands with music and beauty, inviting the unwary to abandon their cares and drown in wanton revelry. I wonder if that is only what the gentry want us to believe, lest we all vanish into fairy land, never to work their ships or land again.

When my woman's blood comes, it feels like the world shifts, sending everything off kilter. Ma says it was once a symbol of power, a ward against the fae on the most dangerous of nights. The preacher decries her folk beliefs. It marks my original sin—I am a filthy woman, there by the grace of the Lord.

"If I climb yer back, will you tak me away, somewhere better'n here?" I ask in whispered tones. But his gaze is impenetrable and his intentions beyond my ken.

Coming of age means thoughts of a future outside Badbae, talk of husbands and babies and womanhood. I feel like a fox being hunted from the undergrowth, dazed and confused, searching for the right path to take.

Da's favourite place in our house is a spot by the fire, dram of home-distilled whisky in his grasp. He lifts his cup to me and smiles, skin creasing at the corners of his sea-beaten eyes. "Ye'll hae yersel' a fine lad and escape this godfersaken place. Jist you see, ma bonnie lass."

But I struggle to believe. These moors are my cursed birthright and escape seems as untouchable as the moon's reflection on the water.

▽

My Da was brought up a farmer. His hands were calloused from working a till, his mind well-versed in the rhythms of the soil and the crop.

He was no true sailor. When men bring news that he is lost at sea, I'm not even surprised—it's like waiting for an axe to swing down and finally hearing the thump of the blade. Herring keeps us fed, but the water is as treacherous as a kelpie, waiting for you to drop your guard so it can pull you under. Losing someone to the sea is just a part of life on the edge of the world.

A lump grows in my throat and I try to swallow it back. My limbs tremble as I contemplate bedtime without his voice in my ear. Ma collapses before me, grief consuming her strength, leaving her as weak as the summer breeze. She expels her sorrow into the peat-smoke air. She sings the lament of the lost lover, while my brothers square their shoulders against the weight of familial responsibility.

I run from the oppressive room, escaping into a cool grey mist.

I run to the moors, where no one will find me. My tears mix with the damp air and anguish burns my throat.

He stands there waiting for me. Eighteen hands of gleaming muscle, his coat slick and shining black like the midnight sky. His rear feet are swallowed in the burn. The steel eyes watch me, unblinking, unwavering. A flick of his ear forms a question, though no sound escapes his velvet lips.

"The sea took my Da." Of course it did. The sea, like the land, is unforgiving and heartless. The words fracture in my mouth, cutting at my throat. I drop to my knees and curl my body downward, a woodlouse trying to hide from stamping boots.

He abandons his sanctuary and steps toward me, head bowed low in supplication. Panic fills my breast but he jerks his head in a brief shake of equine reassurance. He lowers his nose and it brushes against my cheek. I smell the salt air and the aftertaste of rain and the sweet scent of primrose.

"Will you drown me now?" I ask.

He stamps a hoof, tail swishing through the air. His warm breath is like sun breaking through the clouds. I lift my hands to brush the soft hair of his muzzle. He presses his muzzle closer then shifts his legs, lowering his body into the heather. I press my forehead against the curve of his neck and I dream of the old days, when the clans protected your family and gifts to the fae might guarantee your prosperity.

More people come from Auchencraig as the summer draws to a close. Lonely refugees dispossessed of their land for the good of another landlord. They spend long days hauling rocks from the earth, building houses to shelter them against winter's onslaught. The preacher speaks scripture to remind them of the Lord's love, as if that will somehow fill the empty hole where their home used to be.

I watch them fight to make their mark on an unforgiving land. Once, my father would have helped them build; my mother would have shared our food or offered our outgrown clothes. Ma would have laughed and joked, always one to lighten the moment. Without Da, everything in her world is dark. She navigates life in a stupor, mind lost in the sea with her lover.

Winter is tightening its grip on the land when I go to him once more. I scramble over rocks, body hunched forward, hood lifted over my head to protect me from the worst of the gales. The sun is setting and the world is bathed in an amber glow.

He waits for me by the water. A gleaming obsidian guardian of the moors, head held proud in the air. His mind as distant and alien as the stars. A zephyr lifts his mane, but the wind is not his master.

I stand before him, indecision creasing my brow.

"I'm sorry," I say.

These cliffs are no home for us. The weather fights us at every turn, seeking to force us inward to lands where we're not welcome. My brother says there are better lands; more welcoming shores. A ship will be sailing from Cromarty and our family will sail with it, to somewhere we might call home. It is a long walk, carrying all that we can on our backs, but we cannot stay here, waiting to die with Da.

He tosses his nose and huffs out a breath, as dispassionate as always. He stays in place, tethered to the rippling burn. His eyes penetrate my soul, leaving me open and exposed. I lift a hand and place it on his nose, warm and velvet beneath my fingers.

"Would I die if I stayed with you?"

He has no answer, makes no attempt to offer one. My stomach churns and uncertainty clenches around my heart, every beat sounding like a bell in my ears.

"Will it be better there?"

He lifts his foreleg and stamps it into the earth. I move closer and press my chest against his muzzle. His body radiates the warmth of a fire, chasing the chill from my limbs. *I could stay here forever, with him.*

In the distance, my name echoes through the air, once more disturbing our moment.

I close my eyes, building the willpower to move. I step back, fingers drifting across his neck, extending our connection, delaying the moment when his warmth is gone forever. *Why don't you just take me?*

But he doesn't move. He stands sentinel on the edge of our village, bound to my ancestral land in a way denied to me. The last thing I see before I turn away, tears burning my eyes, is his head lifted proudly in the air, unbroken, untamed.

A Thousand Miles West of the Atlantic

by Audrey T. Carroll

I thought the road
a river—a trick
of the eye, a flash
of a moment forgetting
that there is no water
here save for gooselakes

slipping through
time and place to other rivers
         other oceans
         other lands that feel
more like home

Here: only fields of soy and corn, and a harvest
that makes me too sick to speak

All True Love is Sacrifice

by Maggie Nerz Iribarne

I had not expected the lack of people, or all the animals. I *had* expected the rain and cold, even in summer. No, I didn't miss boiling Boston one bit. I zipped my own jacket then Ryan's, his boney body enduring my touch while he stared over my shoulder.

"So, Ry, this is a fairy fort!" I said, vague thoughts of Stonehenge skittering across my mental screen. I led my son by hand along the path, arriving at a large circular indentation edged by an earthen bank. Trees stood in a line along the far edge, watching, their trunks and branches reaching up for storm clouds. Sheep and goats crowded us, nosing the grass, constantly munching.

Ryan's earlier anxiety noises and movements had ceased. On the bus he'd stimmed by rubbing both his thighs, rocking back and forth. Across from us, three older tourist ladies took sharp little glances our way before focusing purposefully out their clouded windows. I felt their eyes on us as we disembarked, choosing to avoid the vacation buzzkill of our existence by remaining on the bus, heading to the next site.

Walking along the stretch of putting green grass, we approached the indentation, peering into it. Piled stones signified something had been built here long ago and dissolved, like teeth in a green gum.

Ryan smiled, patted a sheep. I sat on a rock and checked my phone. No service. The rain continued misting.

"Mornin', ma'am!" I jumped, turned to find a tweedy man in wellies posed on a cane.

He didn't introduce himself, launched into what I imagined was his canned fairy fort spiel. With a straight face he told me we stood in an ancient dwelling space now inhabited by spirits. Apparently there are at least 45,000 of these places in Ireland.

"That's a lot of fairies," I said.

"People birthed here, lived and died here," he said. "Only animals remain. Aye, and the Good People, the spirits. They've protected, some say haunted, this place for generations, and they'll continue doing so, they will."

Ryan now stood in the center of the circular fort. I secured my hood.

"Happy as a pig in muck," the man said.

"We've been here for over a week. Dublin was a little busy. I—"

"No. I mean to say your boy's happy *here*."

Indeed, Ryan's fingers waved like wands. His face tilted skyward, dark hair stringy and in need of a cut, matted against pale skin.

"Ah. He must hear the fairy music, the most beautiful music ever made. Not everyone can hear it. Only special people. Not me. But mind you don't touch the fairy tree, the hawthorn. It kills. Don't cut it. And don't stay here past one AM," the man said, eyes glued on Ryan.

"Fairy music? Trees?"

I turned to face the man, but he was gone.

And Ryan was no longer in view. The animals nudged me along, their steps silent on green velvet. I called for him, feeling a growing unease. I peered again into the fortress. I heard only the patter of rain, a growing wind, the bleating of sheep. My hair hung sopping around my face. I was so cold. *When the hell was the bus coming back? Was it coming back?* I was beginning to panic.

Then, a new noise.

I have to say, one might not know what it's like to have never heard your own child speak. I had dreamt of it, desired it with an intensity I cannot fully admit, to anyone, even to myself. My son, my Ryan, emerged from the fairy fort, almost as though he was floating. I know how this sounds, but he seemed to *glow*. He turned, spun, danced to some magical sound my ears could not enjoy. I squatted to ground myself, otherwise I thought I might pass out. All of the speech lessons and interventions and late night phone conversations to my mother and sister, all the fear and pain of the last ten years fast forwarded to this moment. *Was I dreaming?* Ryan was dancing and laughing. I didn't care.

It became ridiculously late. At ten o'clock Ryan remained in his spell without rest or food. Finally, he stopped moving and grew very still. His eyes lost the wild over-stimulated look they'd sustained to that point and took a purposeful expression. I held my breath, not knowing what to expect.

The trees waited with me.

Then, it happened. His voice came through, husky, rough, unused.

My hands and arms and legs and even my face trembled, an earthquake emerging from my core.

The whole world leaned in, trembled with me. The moon glowed overhead.

"Ta," Ryan said, nodding, "Ta."

Yes, in Irish. *Yes*, Ryan said *Yes*.

I put a hand over my mouth, afraid to break the spell.

He resumed his laughing, his dancing and jumping, and now he was shouting other words I could not deduce, but words just the same.

My watch read 12 AM. Fearing the man's warning, I latched onto Ryan's arm, pulling him with all my might, dragging him from the trees out to the road. When we arrived mud-spattered and soaked at our inn, it was a miracle the owner didn't lock us out. I suppose she took pity on us, troubled as we were.

I've heard that the best journey takes you home, but our return did not soothe. Six months after the fairy fort incident, I watched from the window as Ryan climbed on the short bus, slow and sad, his shoulders rounded. The winter sky was as grey as that Irish one, but it held no mystery, no promise of drenching rain. It was as flat and cold as the colorless ground. I turned to my screen and all the work awaiting me there. Ryan's cracked iPad lay on the desk beside my keyboard. The previous week he'd thrown it against a wall, then he'd shoved a teacher. At home that night he'd hit me.

I endlessly googled the words *fairies, fairy forts, Ireland*. Everything sounded nonsensical, leprechaun stuff to satisfy the average crazy person. I'd seen them all a hundred times by now. I considered exercising, throwing something in the crockpot, watching *Good Morning, America*. I called my sister.

"What's up with you?" she said. "Are you *more* depressed?" We'd often joked about depression being our baseline.

"I'm having trouble getting back in the swing."

"Back in the swing?"

"Since Ireland."

"Sheesh. I wouldn't have given you that trip if I'd known you'd be all screwed up," she joked.

Each day passed in this kind of uncomfortable fog. One fact tugged relentlessly: My boy had spoken. My boy danced and laughed and transformed before my eyes. My silent boy said *Ta, Yes*, to someone. I didn't know who. In Ireland.

One cold grey morning I opened my nightstand drawer and took out my grandmother's rosary beads. I'd never said the prayer. They were just a memory of her life, her time, long ago. I held them, tried to find the words of the Hail Mary. The red crystal beads flashed, picking up some strand of light. A sign? Since when did I believe in such things? Since Ireland. I blinked and the beads became heavy, dull in my hand.

I knelt beside the bed, crouching, pushing my body into the mattress, my head in my hands.

How to pray? How to pray? Just talk.

"I can't do this anymore. Help us," I said, not sure what I meant, not exactly.

▽

Headlights expose the enclosure.

I endure the driver's crinkled rearview eyebrows.

"Here? You want me to drop ya here? Now?"

I nod. Ryan turns his attention to a circle, the shimmering trees around it.

"I can't, Mrs. Not now. No. I won't do it."

"I promised him. My son loves it here. Look at him. We're going to sleep under the stars."

Ryan's face pushes into the window.

"Stars? In this weather?"

"We've been here before. We want to relive it."

"At this hour? It t'isn't right, Mrs. T'isn't."

Accepting my resolution, he sighs, relents.

So much for the Irish believing their stories.

The taillights dwindle in the darkness. Ryan runs to the circle. The trees stand tall and straight and strong, still watching. I follow my son slowly, revering the sheep and goats keeping guard of the space.

And so it is.

That night I hear my son's voice for the second time in his and my life.

Again, he says, "Ta!" Again, his rising ringing laughter. This time, he sings some song, snippets of ancient Irish meeting my ears, an incoherent logorrhea. The leaves shake as though the trees themselves are dancing with my boy. Within their stronghold I see only darkness, but I do not doubt their presence. The Good People accept my offer. My son's voice fades as they escort him to the other, better side. With shaking, deliberate hands, I snap a piece of the hawthorn branch, recline in the cool soft blanket of grass outside the trees. I offer up my story to the multitudes lingering here, whispering in the wind and rain, awaiting the ears who can hear them.

And now my own time has come.

Midsummer Rising I, 2023
mixed media, by Lee Allane

Homebound

by Elizabeth Kerlikowske

Small as the ball we played jacks with,
your world can be palmed or hidden in your pocket.
Its marbled continents tread water as you search
for that neon star that says *You Are Here*. 24 hours
disappear under your bed. The calendar plays musical
chairs with its days. Meals on Wheels shows up hot,
randomly delivered by a man with one bad eye.
You spend hours examining the ball, familiar as
an old high school face almost remembered.
People you don't recognize know your name;
you hold the ball tighter, life compressed, great
blue masses move over lava fields, you see it all,
round in your palm, unsure continents, deceptive
seas, what a world, what a world.

Moonlight, 2021
digital photography, by Elayna Mae Darcy

The Healer Said

by C. Brennecke

It's gonna take time.

How much time?

All of it.

Is it even worth it then?

Every moment is worth its journey,
even the bad,
and especially the good.

Stitches

by Ashling Meehan-Fanning

A cunning woman told me I have lived too many lives,
that my soul has been around too long, was too worn
to function. "There's whistling through yer lungs
where yer blood should be," she told me, the pillars
of her teeth stacked against her blackened gums,
"Yer bones ain't nothing but red twine and rowan twigs."

That cunning woman cut open my chest with a gray wet stone,
my head with a mortar and pestle. She looked at my heart and
traced its lines like an ivy grown agrestal. She tried
to cauterize it, her pale wrinkled hand steady with the flame,
but the wild growth of my insides lapped up the burn
in a lavish frenzy. My brain she took out and with yellowing eyes
examined its folds like pages. The cunning woman took half
and ground it into paste, rubbed it into my gums
with hope that this time wisdom would stick.

My intestines she said were rotted with drink. She replaced them
with prairie grass and dandelions. She gave me bird beaks for fingernails,
dried roots as hair before finally stitching me up, the scar a jagged
constellation.

Surely I was never meant to live this long.
I asked her what I should do, how to make it stop:

"Just keep on livin'," she said, grit between her teeth, "One day yer bound to
get it right."

Our Stars

A.J.M. Aldrian

A.J.M. Aldrian is a graduate of Hamline University with a BFA in Creative Writing, and a minor in History. She loves many genres including fiction; horror, sci-fi, literary, and fantasy, as well as poetry and non-fiction, historical, and nature and memoir. She collects books and loves spending time cuddled up reading them with her partner and cat. She can also be found on her podcast *Thinking on the Air* on Spotify.

To learn more about her work, visit **ajmaldrian648.wixsite.com/my-site**.

Aldrian's work appears on pages 4–5.

Lee Allane

Lee Allane is a writer, visual artist, and performance poet living in the UK. His written work has appeared in a wide range of mainstream publications (from *Penthouse* to *Hotshoe* and *Forum* to *NOW magazine*) and he has had four books published by Thames and Hudson. His first solo art exhibition was in the Woodstock Gallery, London, followed by solo shows in the UK and to a lesser extent Europe. His artwork has also featured in a number of mixed exhibitions, including the Royal Academy, the Royal Birmingham Society of Arts, and the Pastel Society and New English Art Club at the Mall Galleries, London. Prior to the COVID lockdowns he was also part of a jazz combo performing 'spoken word/music' in venues throughout the UK.

To learn more about his work, visit **leeallane.com**.

Allane's work appears on page 66.

Caroline Ashley

Caroline Ashley is a clinical psychologist who works for the NHS in Scotland. She primarily writes fantasy stories with the occasional foray into sci-fi and horror. Caroline publishes a monthly blog about the psychology within storytelling on her website, where you can also find her other published work.

To learn more about her work, visit **carolineashley.co.uk**.

Ashley's work appears on pages 50–57.

James Bosley

James Bosley's poems have been published in *New Letters* and *Indigo*, and a short story in *Gemini*. His plays have been published, translated, and produced in theaters across this land and abroad, including most recently *Chiquita*, which won the Audience Award at the Downtown Urban Arts Festival. He has enjoyed residencies at Yaddo, the MacDowell Colony, and the Edward Albee Foundation. James Bosley's screenplay for his adaptation of his stage play, *Fun*, was nominated for an Independent Spirit Award.

James Bosley's works appear on pages 20 and 21.

Audrey T. Carroll

Audrey T. Carroll is the author of *What Blooms in the Dark* (ELJ Editions, 2024), *Parts of Speech: A Disabled Dictionary* (Alien Buddha Press, 2023), and *In My Next Queer Life, I Want to Be* (kith books, 2023). Her writing has appeared in Lost Balloon, CRAFT, JMWW, Bending Genres, and others. She is a bi/queer/genderqueer and disabled/chronically ill writer. She serves as a Fiction Editor for *Chaotic Merge Magazine*.

She can be found at **audreytcarrollwrites.weebly.com**.

Carroll's work appears on page 58.

Sean Hanrahan

Sean Hanrahan (he, him, his) is the author of the full-length collections *Safer Behind Popcorn* (2019, Cajun Mutt) and *Ghost Signs* (2023, Alien Buddha) and the chapbooks *Hardened Eyes on the Scan* (2018, Moonstone) and *Gay Cake* (2020, Toho). His work has been included in various anthologies and journals. He has taught courses on Chapbooks, Ekphrastic Poetry, and Poetry and the Body. He hosts a monthly poetry series for Moonstone.

He can be found on Instagram as **@gaycakepoet**.

Hanrahan's works appear on pages 48 and 49.

Maggie Nerz Iribarne

Maggie Nerz Iribarne is 54, lives in Syracuse, NY, writes about witches, cleaning ladies, priests/nuns, the very very old, struggling teachers, neighborhood ghosts, and other things.

She keeps a portfolio of her published work at **maggienerziribarne.com**.

Iribarne's work appears on pages 59–65.

Elizabeth Kerlikowske

Elizabeth Kerlikowske's most recent book is *The Vaudeville Horse* (Etchings Press, 2022). She wrote the text for *Art Speaks: Paintings and Poetry* (Kazoo Books, 2018) with painter Mary Hatch, an ekphrastic adventure. She also creates visual art. An arts activist, she is past-president of the Kalamazoo Friends of Poetry and of the Poetry Society of Michigan.

Kerlikowske's works appear on pages 7 and 67.

Neethu Krishnan

Neethu Krishnan is a writer based in Mumbai, India. She holds an MA in English and an M.Sc. in Microbiology, and writes between genres at the moment. Her work has appeared in twenty-seven international literary venues including *The Spectacle*, *Fu Review*, *The Saltbush Review*, and elsewhere, and is forthcoming in more. She is a Best of the Net poetry nominee and recipient of Bacopa Literary Review's Creative Nonfiction Award. She also has a poem published in *The Polaris Trilogy*, which is slated for a 2024 NASA launch to the moon.

You can find her on Instagram at **@neethu.krishnan_**.

Krishnan's work appears on page 1.

Aaron Lelito

Aaron Lelito is a visual artist and writer from Buffalo, NY. His images have been published as cover art in *Red Rock Review*, *Peatsmoke Journal*, and *The Scriblerus*. His poetry chapbook *The Half Turn* was published in 2023, and his work has also appeared in *Barzakh Magazine*, *Novus Literary Arts Journal*, *SPECTRA Poets*, *The Primer*, and *Santa Fe Review*. He is editor in chief of the art & literature website *Wild Roof Journal*.

Find more of his work at **aaronlelito.com**.

Lelito's work appears on page 10.

Aimee Lowenstern

Aimee Lowenstern (she/her) is a twenty-five year old poet living in Nevada. She has cerebral palsy and a chihuahua. Her work can be found in several literary journals, including *Fifth Wheel Press* and *The Bombay Literary Magazine*.

You can find her on X as **@everyepithet**.

Lowenstern's work appears on pages 46–47.

Ashling Meehan-Fanning

Ashling Meehan-Fanning is a poet based in Madison, Wisconsin. She is working on finishing her MFA in poetry at Augsburg University in Minnesota. Her collection *Colossal Girl* was self-published in December 2020. Her recent work has been featured in *Troublemaker Firestarter Vol. 4*, *Thó Wiŋ Magazine*, *Written Tales*, and *The Crackling Kettle*.

To learn more about her work, visit **poemsbyashling.com**.

Meehan-Fanning's works appear on pages 19 and 32–33.

dora morrigan

dora morrigan is an amateur poet who recently released her debut collection of poetry titled *What There Was (Or What There Wasn't)* through Dalygood Media. The book is available now through all major retailers. She is also published through AZE Journal and Elixir Verse Press.

You can continue to follow her work on her website **dalygoodmedia.com**.

morrigan's work appears on pages 8–9.

Christopher R. Muscato

Christopher R. Muscato is a writer from Colorado, USA. He is the former writer-in-residence of the High Plains Library District, with work appearing in *Shoreline of Infinity*, *Solarpunk Magazine*, and *House of Zolo*, among other places.

Muscato's work appears on pages 22–30.

Charlotte Amelia Poe

Charlotte Amelia Poe (they/them) is an autistic nonbinary author from England. Their first book, *How To Be Autistic*, was published in 2019. Their debut novel, *The Language of Dead Flowers*, was published in September 2022. Their second memoir, *Conversations with Monsters*, will be published in 2024. Their poetry has been published internationally.

To learn more about their work, visit **charlottepoe.com**.

Poe's work appears on pages 10–11.

Lorraine Schein

Lorraine Schein is a New York writer and poet. Her work has appeared in *VICE Terraform*, *Strange Horizons*, *Scientific American*, *NewMyths*, and *Michigan Quarterly*, and in the anthologies *Wild Women* and *Tragedy Queens: Stories Inspired by Lana del Rey & Sylvia Plath*. *The Futurist's Mistress*, her poetry book, is available from Mayapple Press. Her book *The Lady Anarchist Cafe* is out now from Autonomedia.

The Lady Anarchist Cafe is available at **autonomedia.org/product/the-lady-anarchist-cafe**.

Schein's work appears on pages 2–3.

Sarena Tien

Sarena Tien is a queer Chinese American writer and feminist. Once upon a time, she used to be so shy that two teachers once argued whether she was a "low talker" or "no talker," but she's since learned how to scream. Her poetry and prose have appeared in publications such as *Bustle*, *Decoded Pride*, *The Rumpus*, *Snarl*, and *Sylvia*.

Tien's work appears on pages 16–18.

Odi Welter

Odi Welter (they/she/he) is a queer, neurodivergent author currently studying Film and Creative Writing at the University of Wisconsin-Milwaukee. They have been published in several magazines such as *Yellow Arrow Vignette*, *Hamilton Arts and Letters*, and *Broken Antler Quarterly*. When not writing, they are indulging in their borderline unhealthy obsessions with fairy tales, marine life, superheroes, and botany.

Find them on Instagram at **@o.d.i.welter**.

Welter's work appears on pages 12–13.

Anne Wheeler

Anne Wheeler grew up with her nose in a book but earned two degrees in aviation before it occurred to her that she was allowed to write the stories that had been brewing in her head for years. When not writing her next novel, she can be found planning her next escape to the desert or anywhere with an elevation above 8000 feet—camera gear included. A commercial pilot, aircraft mechanic, jet engine geek, and occasional flight instructor, she lives in Georgia with her husband, son, and herd of cats.

You can find her on Instagram at **@annewheelerphotos**.

Wheeler's works appear on pages 6 and 21.

Claudia Wysocky

Claudia Wysocky, a Polish poet based now in New York, is known for her ability to capture the beauty of life through rich descriptions in her writing. She firmly believes that art has the potential to inspire positive change. With over five years of experience in fiction writing, Claudia has had her poems published in local newspapers and magazines. For her, writing is an endless journey and a powerful source of motivation.

Wysocky's work appears on pages 14–15.

Our Editors

C. Brennecke

C. Brennecke is a multimedia artist, writer, and editor hailing from the suburbs of Philadelphia and currently residing in Metro Detroit. She's a proud alum of Temple University and a founding editor at Elixir Verse Press. Her passions include art, Tarot, feng shui, exclaiming every time she sees a dog, and any creative outlet that lets her put her imagination to work. She's also an avid cuddler and sushi eater, and thinks that she could one day go pro in either sport.

Follow her projects at **mythsmistsmusings.com**.

Brennecke's work appears on pages 31 and 69.

Elayna Mae Darcy

Elayna Mae Darcy is a queer poet, filmmaker, and star cluster of feelings. They are the author of the *Unveil Me* poetry duology and *Still The Stars*, a YA space fantasy novel in verse that is the first book in a planned trilogy. She also has had an array of short works published in literary magazines that include *just femme & dandy*, *Wizards in Space Literary Magazine*, and *Impostor Lit*. Their favorite being in the universe is their black cat, Bean.

Follow their works at **elaynamusings.com**.

Darcy's work appears on pages iv, 34, 35, 45, and 68.

Guest Editor

Christina Rosso

Christina Rosso (she/they) is a writer, educator, and bookstore owner living outside of Philadelphia with her bearded husband and rescue pups. She is the author of *Creole Conjure* (Maudlin House, 2021) and *She Is A Beast* (APEP Publications, 2020). Their writing has been nominated for Best of the Net, Best Small Fictions, and the Pushcart Prize. Currently, she teaches in the humanities department at Moore College of Art. When Christina isn't teaching or working at the bookstore, they read tarot and cast spells under the full moon.

For more information, visit **christina-rosso.com**.

Rosso's work appears on pages 36–44.

Coming Soon...

ELIXIR VERSE EQUINOX

Stella Verses ★ Fall 2024

Elixir Verse Press is an indie literary press, founded in 2023 by two poets who have dedicated their lives to stories and the stars. In addition to publishing works that vary from the whimsical to the primordial, we strive to be a hub of community where like-minded and open-hearted authors can connect, encourage, and inspire one another.

We believe that when writing is partnered with community, the result is truly magical. Together with our friends, literary contacts, and YOU, we're endeavoring to create a thriving community that serves writers and readers alike.

For more information, explore
elixirversepress.com